The Absent Word

Tahleah Fisher

BookLeaf
Publishing

Presentation by *BookLeaf Publishing*

Web: www.bookleafpub.com

E-mail: info@bookleafpub.com

ISBN: 9789357445221

First edition 2021

DEDICATION

For my mother.

THERENESS

TODAY I HAD A WEIRD MOMENT,
While I was thinking of things, I hated,
WHEN ONE OF MY FRIENDS ASKED
WHAT WAS WRONG,
And that was more painful than they thought.

IT WAS A PECULIAR SENSE OF
THERENESS,
Something I couldn't quite grasp,
LIKE IF SHE OFFERED TO GIVE ME A
HUG, OR BE CLOSE,
As she had done,

THE GLASS AROUND MY FEELINGS,
CRACKED WITH SIMPLE PRESSURE.
I was never quite alone,
I HAD PEOPLE THAT WERE THERE FOR
ME,
They asked daily if I was okay, and said they
loved me, held me,

BUT THEN,
Why?
I NEVER TELL THEM OF AN INNER
SECRET, OF THINGS THAT MAKE ME CRY,

In the middle of the night, during the day,

SOMETIMES I'LL BE SITTING ON THE
SAME COUCH, SILENT, UNNOTICED,
Too many excluded issues that swarm them,
devour them,
I WONDER IF FOLDING BACK THE
CORNERS I HAVE KEPT IN ME,
Will do nothing but litter their security with
paper cuts,

TO WATCH THEM BLEED, TO PITY THE
BLOOD-STAINED CORNERS,
I could never live with myself,
YET THAT THERENESS, THE PROMISE
THAT "YOU'LL BE OKAY",
"we are there for you, even when we don't think
it's needed"

IT'S A THERENESS, THAT MAKES ME
FEEL JUST A LITTLE LESS ALONE.
And that thereness is more important than a
touch that makes me break

Why Do We Cry?

And they asked him,
"Why do you hesitate,"
"To name what is known?"
And he whispered,
"When all that flies,"
"Looks like an angel,"
"Doesn't the devil,"
"Look like a saint?"

And they prodded him,
"Why must you scream,"
"When no wound has bled?"
And he smiled, and said,
"As a splinter is invisible,"
"And the pain is immense,"
"A wound from a sword,"
"Should cause no pain at all."

And they scowled at him,
"Why do you hide from us,"
"When we have done nothing to you?"
And he cried and he said,
"Why does the rabbit,"
"Frequent the fox's den,"
"Looking for the clover,"

"When they know death is near?"

And they kicked him and screamed,
"Why do you keep walking,"
"When you have nowhere to go?"
And he stood and grinned,
"Why does the ocean caress the sand,"
"Knowing it can't move it?"
"Why does the whale,"
"Beach itself on our lands?"
"Why do we cry,"
"When there's nothing to nourish?"
"Why does a ghost wander among us,"
"When nothing good comes of it?"

And they killed him and glowered,
"How does it feel,"
"When you finally get to die?"
And he rested, for once, and laid there,
"When a stone falls,"
"Into the darkening riverbed,"
"Does the water pause,"
"Or carry on blindly?"

And she stood over him, frowning,
"Why would you do this,"
"Die so easily?"
And he closed his eyes quietly,
"You didn't stop me,"

"So how can a raindrop,"
"Resist the freedom of falling,"
"Without a cloud to cling to?"

So he stood over his love's grave,
"You can come back to life,"
"Only if you were brave enough to try."
And for once, his eyes opened,
"If I came back,"
"Would I be driven away for being undead,"
"Or would I be shunned,"
"For being the same as I was alive?"

And he crouched there, on the dirt,
"They might do both,"
"I cannot be certain,"
And for once, he had nothing to say,
"But if you were to live again,"
"What pride you could have,"
"To say you survived death,"
"Just to prove you weren't to be silenced?"

So he pulled the boy,
Out of his grave to the grass,
He was heavier than he was,
Before everything had happened,
Because the mystery of emptiness,
Is that it is heavier than most.

So he led away the ghost of him,
And brought him back to life,
They ignored the murderers at the door,
In his head, in his home,
And the boy who was dead,
Learned how to breathe for himself.

And he looked at the dead man walking,
"Why did you feel so tired,"
"That you thought you had to die?"
And he smiled for once, a real one,
"Because when people tell you,"
"How you think is wrong,"
"And everything about you is dead,"
"Why not add one more?"

Sweet Relief

My anxiety is a calm ocean with deep currents
My anxiety is a field of empty,
Tall grass, at midnight,

My anxiety is the buzzing undertone of a spoken
word,
A cymbal crash that catches you off-guard,
My anxiety is the chilled winds,
That carries drops of distant rainstorms,

My anxiety is bolts of lightning,
Preserved for eternity in the photographs,
of my memory and inked with my
blackened doubts,

It is the broken car,
Under thin, breaking tree limbs,
The silver of light on the man,
Out of view,

The reflection of his face, in the rear-view
mirror,
It is the rumble of the engine,
The squealing set of tires in thick mud,

Anxiety is the isolated scream that travels for miles,
Speaking of chilled winds and loneliness,
Of an empty casket and funeral rooms,

Because it, too, knows,
Nobody has had that sweet relief,
Of dying, yet.

More Myth, Than Girl

she was papers stained with ink
words scrawled on full notebooks

she was tears shed at Disney movies
covered snickers at stupid jokes

we were crying at early hours of the morning
linking fingers as we promised not to let go

we were apologizing for unsaid words
one's that never even needed them

I was bundles of thoughts
balls of wool tangled with no beginnings

I was ice on windshields
that never melted in the spring

she was the paintings of gods at luxurious suppers
feasting with people that worshipped her

she was the scrap pieces of poetry
that she shoved in envelopes to deliver to me

I was a hopeless romantic
falling in love and weeping unspoken
confessions over her words

I was a locked chest
with too many things to spill

she was the quiet thunderstorm
that raged when we were asleep

she was crashing, howling winds
that rattled windows and stirred our content

we were whispering at midnight
drowning in empty bottles like we wished we
were dead

we were words of distant dreams
that we knew were impossible

I listened like she was a god
and I was nothing more than a disciple

I was, in a way
she spoke words that brought meaning to a
clouds shapes and the raindrops

she was swallowed cries
bitten-back gasps for air

she was a flowing river
grasping at loose pebbles in the banks

she was a cry for help in crowded hallways
a voice, singular, among dozens

she was bruised knuckles
red knees, and quipped words

she was flailing arms
and kicking legs that beat nothing but air

she was suffocating on her thoughts
she was convinced she wasn't here

she was a million things
but we only listened to o n e

she was a myth
nothing more than divine and nothing less

she was not a girl in our eyes
but she was only that

I was blind words and deaf ears

for now she'll be a bird
she will be the first of us to fly alone

but now we are only broken promises
because one of us did let go

and the sad part is

I don't know which one of us it was that did

If I Did As You Told Me

Where would I be today
If I listened to what you told me?
My friend, my confidant,
How much have I exposed to you?
How many wounds did I stretch,
To fit you inside the seams?

I'd be tucking myself in,
Under six feet of dirt and grime.
With the taste of lead on my tongue,
And thoughts muddled beyond repair.
If I took your advice, my friend,
Picked it out of our messages.

It makes me wonder, what if?
Would you go to the funeral?
Would you risk getting thrown out?
Would my family, my mother,
Rub dirt on your name?
Would you accept disgrace?

But this is if I listened,

To all you told me to do,
But I didn't.
    So I wrote about it.

The Girl With No Name

I never could figure it out,
Where the girl had come from.
She was small, pale, afraid,
I noticed how her hands shook.
I can't remember when she found me,
No one ever really saw her,
Until one time the girl kicked and screamed,
And clawed at my wrists until they bled.
Soon enough I grew attached,
We were joined at the hip.
Recently she's grown quite tame,
She'll follow me and hang on words,
I can feel her hovering twenty-four-seven.
Yet some nights she looks less small,
She grows until she looks older than my mum,
She'll perch on my chest and scream.
She'll claw at my skin and repeat words,
Things I've heard before,
Things I've said before, years ago.
Then she'll go quiet, shrink and lay.
She'll lay beside me and stare.
I asked her what she was,

I had asked before, demanded it,
She had recoiled, and whimpered,
"I am you but doubled",
For a moment we'd sit,
"What's your name?" I'd ask,
She'd tell me she didn't care for it.
Others had said her name for me,
Written on typed sheets of paper,
With numbers scrawled on sticky notes,
Sending me to people across town,
To drive her away, to silence her.
I held her shaking face in my hands,
Found the features that mirrored my own,
But younger and more afraid.
I gifted her a new name,
Undid the shackles of our diagnosis,
Freed her as the others wanted,
But I still kept her around.
That day I held my Anxiety,
My doubts and crippling desperation,
And I named her Hope.

Burning Blue

Sit with me, my dear,
Sit with me on our roof,
We alone have tickets,
To the end of the world.
Sit with me and watch,
Watch the sky burn.
Watch the stars hide from us,
Because even they learned.
They learned we weren't the stuff of myths,
Watch the cerulean blue swallow itself,
Watch the clouds chew themselves out,
Watch the people below.
Watch them realize the deliciousness,
Of the despair, of the inevitable,
You ask me "the Question",
"Why does the burn now?"
And I will tell you,
I would say, that all good things,
All things we love, are fleeting.
I would say that each and every thing,
Only has a meaning,
Because humans were desperate.
"What for? What is there to think about?"
There isn't.
We were so scared of never knowing,

Of never believing, of never seeing,
That we pretended the mundane could save us.
"Where's the harm in that?"
The sky is burning, I'd say.
The stars are eating themselves alive,
All for us,
Isn't it beautiful?

I Made A Room For You In My Mind

i made a room for you in my mind,
it is full of things you might not like,
but they remind me of you.
it has bushels of wildflowers,
in glass vases in every corner,
there are wide open windows.
and the image of you there stretches,
each morning kissed by the sunlight.
there's a bathroom ensuite,
and stacks of books in every space,
i see you tripping over every word.
i see you staring at those flowers.
you do this almost everyday.
what hurts the most is,
you never see your image in the mirror,
that i'd placed hoping you'd see.
so you could see that morning beauty,
that creases around your eyes,
the smile that i always see.
you never look into your own eyes,
i'd hoped you'd see the face i saw.
what hurts even more,

is that heart of mine,
i've hidden in a flower vase,
cushioned and cradled by petals,
it beats and pulses,
shaking dewdrops from its veins.
you take one look at it,
listen briefly to the earnest whispers,
of every thought i've had of you.
you plug your ears with thorns,
and throw the rest out the door,
they bleed and i bleed,
and my heart clenches on my porch.
at night i wonder if your ears are still plugged,
if you can hear my words through the walls,
do you hear me right now?
how much love i hold for you?
how many times i speak your praises?
does the mention of your name on my lips,
rouse you from your dreamless sleep?
i have already laid my heart,
my soul, out bare for you.
they have trembled in my hands,
first you smiled at me,
soothed the petals over the mess,
you lovingly tended to the blossom,
not even days later,
had the whispering driven you insane,
i know i am a foolish person,
a mockery of a greenhouse,

the flowers within are wilted, but,
am i foolish to believe you'll open the door?
open it just for me?

Incorrigible

i learned a new word today
it was the word incorrigible
it meant to be unwilling
unwilling to change or be better

i heard it in my favorite musical
watching it with my mother last night
even the characters didn't know of it
i wonder,
could i use the word for you
    my friend?

Alone Vs. Lonely

when i am sitting on my bed,
it's peaceful, i'm alone,
and i am happy,

when i remove myself from conversations,
i am safe, i am alone,
and i am happy,

when mum is asleep,
and i am suffering, i am lonely,

when she is sicker than usual,
and i am helpless, i am lonely

when my friends refuse to reply,

when i am ignored when i need them,

when i am abandoned and forgotten,
because i missed the status quo,

when i realize i haven't overcome,
anything that plagued me,

i may not be alone,
but i am more lonely

All My Missed Calls

I had nine missed calls
One after another
Each early in the morning
Attached to messages.

My mother was the first to call
She bid me good luck in all endeavors
Said she was proud of me, always
I thanked her, for everything she had faith in
I thanked her, though she couldn't see.

My father was after her then
He had stolen my number
From family-friends and extended members
He asked me for a dozen things
I sent him a single message
"I'm sorry I wasn't the daughter you wanted"
And then I blocked him
He was dead to me then.

The rest of my family followed
One person relaying all their messages

They all said the same thing
What I did was boring, useless
I would never be enough
Never worth the effort to call
Unless I was needed or Christmas rolled around.

My old friends came next
They were all the same really
They blended and blurred into one person
They told me my life wasn't worth it
They told me they didn't need me
They never did though
I was a fool to believe they did
It wished me the best and ended
I had stopped answering them years ago.

My cousin B next
I missed his call on accident
He rambled about a story
Something of mine he wished to read
He is too young now but he will be soon
He was happy now and then
I called him back
Just to say I loved him.

My brother called at dawn
He sat in silence for hours
On multiple calls, or attempts
Then he called me by those words

"My sister", I knew he knew that too
I saw him post about me on Facebook
Though he spelled my name wrong
And he only spoke to me as a baby
Over the phone the first time
We spoke again, a few years later
We were still practically strangers
"I hope we can fix it."

My sister called when her daughter woke
Her daughter did most of the talking
She told me many stories about them both
She used words I couldn't understand yet
Spoke of a culture I had long forgotten
I sent my sister a message later
"Thank you."

The next person I didn't know
I don't know what they were to me
They told me of different lives
Of homes in countries I longed to see
They told me everything was moving
That they knew I was afraid
And that was okay
I would be okay.

The final person who called was me
I said only a few words
"We are growing. We are natural"

"We are alive. Thank you for trying"
I never thought I'd hang up on myself
I didn't mean to ignore myself

(No one had called that morning,
No one cared to hear my voice,
To know how I was coping with things,
I was alone to deal with things,
And I was still okay.)

all the god's that weren't mine

i believe that from a young age athena has blessed me. she has hovered, gifted me the idea that i know more than i should, and this makes me think. to think, i wonder, is a blessing and a curse. i both loathe her and adore her for this. i am filled with words, that bubble, boil over, and they burn when i cough them up. sometimes they are too quiet to hear, it is then i feel her disappointment in me.

i praise artemis at night. all things beautiful and dark. wild, ever-growing, moon-kissed and forever young, untouched. she is the world of things i have sometimes found myself ignoring. i do not hear from her most nights. except when i find myself awake at night, when the darkness is suffocating, and the moon is watching me from her perch - selene has always been close to me. artemis sits with me. i can hear her in the soft breathing of the cat perched on my covers. she sits, and she says nothing, but she is there.

i ask apollo often for the ability to find some semblance of order in my written word.
sometimes he sits atop my shoulder and strums a tune, sings a melody that lulls me into a daze, enough to take control of the words i have.
he never stays long. but i leave hidden messages in my stories for him, try a little harder with my music, my poetry, so he knows i am thankful.

dionysus is a god i've thought of briefly. what he is and represents are all the things i could dream of. i wish to dance around fires, drinking down my desires, choking on the idea that "yes, we are alive".
he is carefree and devastatingly happy. i want to be like him, but the opportunity to take a sip from the chalice of those thoughts also terrifies me. the woods are too dark, and the fires are too distant it seems.

aphrodite is a different story.
she comes the most often. though she is always small, and only when it is quiet, when i catch myself in the reflections, when my head runs dry of fruitful thoughts. she is beautiful. she lays with me, whispers all the things i wish to hear, she tells me i am beautiful.
i am flesh and blood, stardust and red-hot, liquid gold, i am satin smoothness and jagged edges. i

am contradictory and so perfect in that sense.
she tells me this and more.
sometimes i find myself succumbing to these
compliments. they are the golden apple of my
chaos. but more often then not, i see her
frowning. her face has become sullen.
i rarely agree with what the lady says.

but what do these things matter, if they were
never mine to begin with.

a letter to my father

there are only three things i can think of
that would be worth my time saying

the first;
"am i a daughter to you?"
you have one already,
perhaps more,
a son too,
was i a daughter or a trophy?
is a child something to boast about?
do you have to many,
to even know my name?

the second;
"do you feel?"
the question is vague,
what do you feel, is better,
regret? sorrow? envy?
pride? indifference?
do you regret failing us enough,
to be ejected from a place,
that had your name engraved?
do you feel sad that i've never,
had the chance to know you?

the last;
"could you be proud of me?"
i hate this question more than anything,
i don't want you to be proud,
i don't want you to be around us,
i just don't want you.
so why?
tell me why it hurts that i've never,
ever heard the words "i'm proud of you"?
at least not from you,
why does it sting, why do i envy,
when i see that no one else has to feel,
the same way that i do?
since when did this become something to feel?

and at last
i have one statement

i hate you
you are no father to me

signed,
me.

not that i care

i had your words on repeat,
not that i care,

things you told me to do to myself,
not that i care,

if i died, you wouldn't watch me buried,
not that i care,

i remembered sitting in my bathtub, hating
myself,
not that i care,

i remember every time someone hurt me,
not that i care,

could feel it in the vibrations of my mind,
not that i care,

i remember wanting to taste lead on my tongue,
not that i care,

i remember the disappointment at missed calls,
not that i care,

i remember watching the driveway for cars that
never came,
not that i care,

i remember thinking that the world would end
tomorrow,
not that i cared,

i remember listening to you tell me i deserved
bad things i got,
not that you cared,

you never cared,
but neither do i,

i do not care,
because to care means i admit that the facts hurt,

to care means i miss you.

time

it is [12:34am]. i sit on my front step. i asked to be here. when the air in my lungs is as heavy as lead. when i feel the thoughts of my brain fall through to my stomach, and constrict the bowels of my body. when the tiny voice in my head has become a screaming thing, a hissing thing, a writhing thing, a thing to be feared, a thing that demands to be the forefront of the stage-play of my mind. it is a jealous thing. it is envious of the fact that my lesser known ministrations have become the protagonist recently. they bite, and we bleed. it doesn't notice that we seep collectively into a cold puddle on the concrete step. where the moon can kiss her own reflection.

it is [2:13am]. i have long since retired to the familiarity of my home. there is nothing but stillness and something calming in the quiet. here the thing in my head is silent. it is dormant. it feels safe, and so it gifts me that security. that same security that it whispers to me that i don't deserve. something we don't even have. it is at this time where the words bleed and they soak through the page. when my words have meaning and i have a reason to convey them.

it is [8:36am]. that horrible thing has returned, baring its teeth, coiling around every screen i own, breathing down my neck as i reply to each and every message i receive. what is it telling me? i can hear it. but i'm drowning, almost, almost. i can see a dozen faces and yet i am alone. i am in a room of people i've known for years and yet i don't know half of them well enough.

it is [2:39pm]. many of the faces i see i knew. once upon a time. at some point. i don't know how we went from one point to another. the thing that has been watching me all day has finally gone passive, lay across my lap and stares at the screen. it knows what they've done. i know what they've done. no matter how many days i hear it asking me, "have we made the mistake of blaming them?" each day we reply "no, we were right, it is painful but that is okay." i have begun to prioritize being right over being safe.

it is [11:00pm]. i am tired of looking. tired of knowing that thing is with me. tired of breathing, eating, drinking, doing, saying, thinking, tired of existing. exhausted by the premise that waking up in the morning is keeping me alive. i'm tired, my bones ache, so i lay beside the thing that haunts me and sleep. ready to do it all again in the morning.

train car

i found a train car filled with people i knew once. knew now. will know. their faces were blurred, blackened, hazy with smog and memory that had failed me. i only had their voices to speak of my memories, to tell me of what they had known of me. i heard buzzy voices of people of my childhood. some told me i was useless. i was defective, unlovable. words as ugly as they had told me i was. some asked if there was something wrong with me. my mother's was the only face i saw. she said nothing was wrong with me, and if there were, i was fine as is. broken things are fixable, but sometimes fixing is painful. i heard words from a man i used to believe i knew. he said things i had once loved. words i had cherished and held close to a guarded place that i never wanted to open. from the inside out i had poisoned myself with those words, and it was only when i was sick that the words found a new tone, when i found that the Devil had looked like an angel once.

i found one face that i remember well. we sat together in silence. neither of us were big talkers. neither were touchy-feely, as we put it,

but we sat together and let the talking rattle the train car. watched the windows fade from one home to another. i told her about the things that happened in each one. things i heard and saw. felt, experienced. she felt sad for me. and soon more faces came into clarity, the ones that cared sat around us. they told me that they cared, through words i couldn't hear, and they offered me sympathy on a plate of shiny silver. it looked as poisonous as the words i had heard before. i was afraid if i looked it would bite. but we placed our hands over the offer, and we were okay. we healed.
the train stopped at our destination.

things i said over the phone

i told a girl i liked her over the phone . we had been friends for a year and a half , maybe a little more , however close to eternity sounded fair . i laid my soul bare in a couple of digital pixels , with a line drawn through it ; one because it was there , two because i couldn't handle looking at those same pitiful words without making it look like i had written them down and crossed them out on paper . i had only liked someone of the same gender as me once before . and that didn't last . i was , and am , young and very unaware . my brain is a maze of things that i do not understand , i cannot understand , maybe i will never understand . she answered the day after , because she never saw it . from there i felt a mixture of relief and hope . for once my spontaneous feelings and inability to word them , and forcing myself to do so , had worked in my favor . until it didn't . i don't blame her for saying no . i don't blame her for being unsure before . i blame myself for allowing myself to betray a holy image i had painted in my head , an image i tainted , an image i could never forgive myself for .

we are still friends now . closer even maybe . i won't admit to her that her touch burns . sitting close enough to me to be on my knee has long since made my stomach eat itself from the inside out . that alone reminds me of the image of her . it burns , and i feel it . but i don't tell her . i don't deserve to quell the pain . perhaps the times she told me things were fine were lies too .

What Happens To Chatty People

i imagine someone asking me,
"what ever happens to chatty people?"
they asked because they knew who i was,
before things i never even told them about.

when i was bright, loud, bubbly,
when friendships were tethered to me,
and i wasn't afraid of letting go.
i was a chatty child once, perhaps,
thinking of it sounds more like a hazy dream.

"what do you think happened to chatty people?"
i ask because i don't know how to answer,
answers hurt, but questions distract.

"i think they ran out of things to talk about."
i didn't tell them, but i knew what happened to
chatty people.

there is a chatty person in your class, workplace,
home, but you can't see them. they sit beside
you, they scream into your ears, tell you all the

things they've seen in a day, all the beautiful things, that they want to share with you, because they love you. but you can't hear them. you have long since placed your hands over your ears. even if you haven't, a glance away, a bored look, a patronizing question, if you have done these, you have flicked a switch on the sound in a person's body. the only voice they have is the one in their head. the only purpose they have to you is a person to listen.

the chatty person has long since accepted the fact that no one is listening.

their words don't matter.

their words don't matter.

their words don't matter.

their words never mattered.

you showed them that more than once.
the chatty person has become what they wanted, someone who listens, and asks no questions. but i won't tell you that in person. you have to figure that our for yourself.

abstract

you sit upside down with me,
on a bench in an art gallery,
we stare at a painting, and we talk about what we see,
to others we sound like we know what it means,
what she means, he? they? it? what?
it's okay that we don't know,
we see our faces in the shiny reflections,
we sit together for hours, staring and thinking,
but the thing is we aren't thinking about the painting,
the painting watches us as we talk about each other.

my mother's heels

my mother used to wear pretty boots,
with heels that clacked when i walked,
i was too young to wear them,
but i would put them on and parade around the kitchen,
clicking and clacking as i went,
so she knew that i was wearing them, and i was proud of it.

my mother used to dress up and go to parties,
she used to go to forget things,
she used to go to have a sliver of semblance of fun,
my mother wore clothes she made herself,
she went and she smiled,
as if there wasn't a black hole in her head.

my mother probably used to cry,
i wouldn't know, i've only seen her cry twice,
maybe three times, of sadness.
my mother shoulders the weight of things handed to her,
and i try to hold what i can of my own,
because a mountain can look like a mole-hill in comparison to the world.

my mother was a lot of things,
my mother is still a lot of things,
she isn't the same things,
but she is my mother,
and i wouldn't ask for any other,
in a way we saved each other when we needed
it,
my mother is a queen and she deserves the
respect she earns.

wanderlust

there is a dirt path outside that i've long ignored. my friends have packed the dirt from years of use. there are wildflowers growing in cracks in the earth. i see her standing at the end, she waits for me, holding out a hand. she tells me that the world is growing. the path is long. it may look daunting, and it does in all honesty, watching the world dip over the bend. but we are growing. we are forever connected to the dirt and the people and the sun.

she asks me what i saw in my reflection when i looked this morning. i said i didn't see myself. "is not-yourself a good or bad thing?" i said i didn't look the same as i had yesterday. but i did not hate what i saw. i looked alive, and that was what made me proud.

i lived, though i was told to die. even when i wanted to burn myself and bury myself, i lived. i woke up, kissed the moon, cherished the sun, went to bed, and did it all again. words failed me, conversations ended, relations ended. i stopped seeing people that i knew would poison me.

i took the hand she gave me. and i accepted the fact that i was healing. and the stretching of the new skin over the old and wounded would hurt, i'd want to give up, i'd miss people i never wanted to. but that's how growing works.

buds come with thorns, light comes with burning, we are born to burn.

www.ingramcontent.com/pod-product-compliance
Lightning Source LLC
Chambersburg PA
CBHW051738130826
49812CB00033B/917
* 9 7 8 9 3 5 7 4 4 5 2 2 1 *